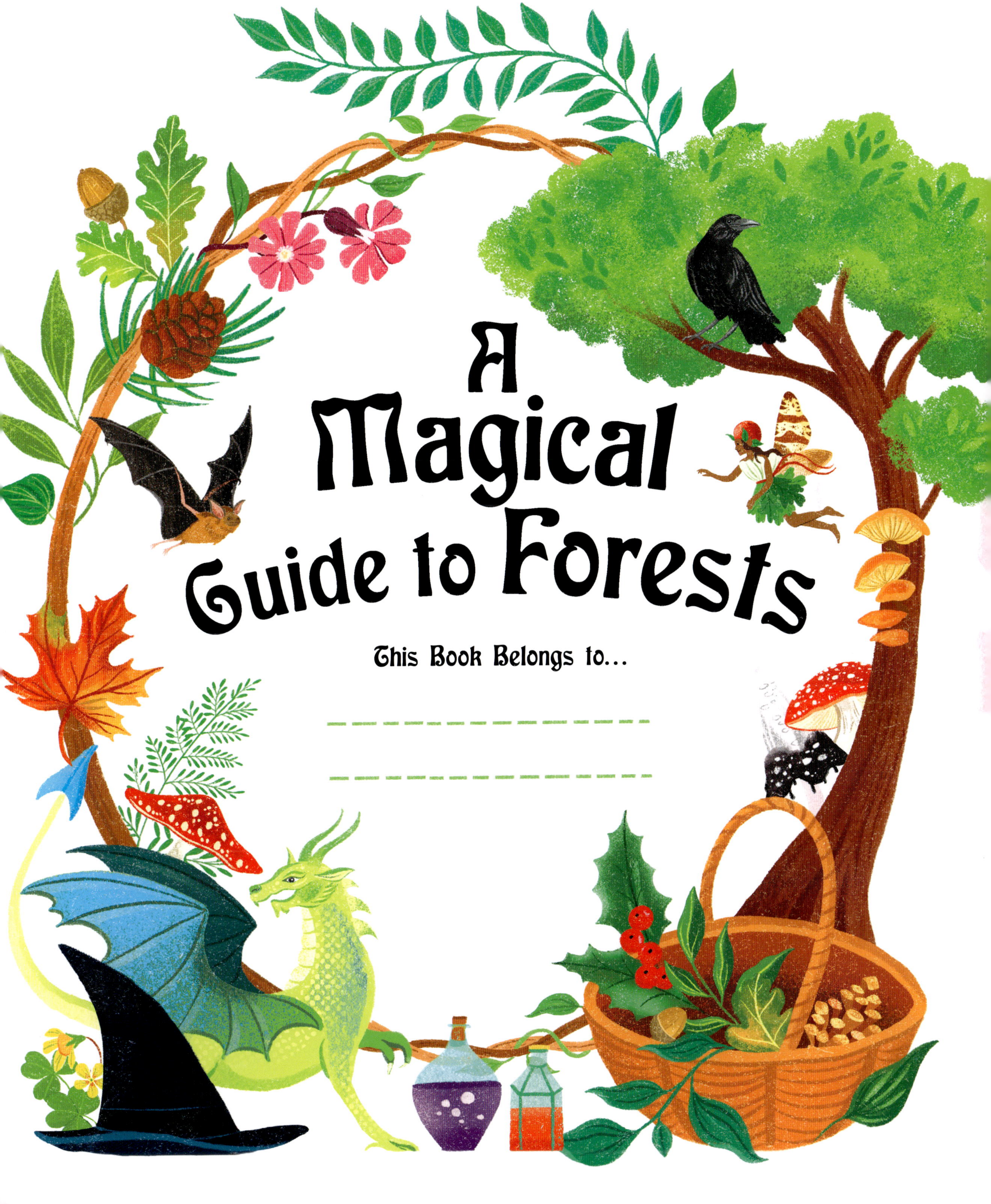
A Magical Guide to Forests
This Book Belongs to...

First published in Great Britain in 2026
by Welbeck Children's Books

A CIP catalogue record for this book is available from the British Library.

HB ISBN: 978-1-8045-3643-8

Printed in China

Welbeck Children's Books
An imprint of Hachette Children's Group,
Part of Hodder and Stoughton Limited
Carmelite House, 50 Victoria Embankment
London EC4Y 0DZ

An Hachette UK Company
www.hachette.co.uk
www.hachettechildrens.co.uk

10 9 8 7 6 5 4 3 2 1

MIX
Paper | Supporting responsible forestry
FSC® C104740

The authorised representative in the EEA is Hachette Ireland,
8 Castlecourt Centre, Dublin 15, D15 XTP3, Ireland (email: info@hbgi.ie)

A Magical Guide to Forests

Folklore, History, and Spells

Sandra Lawrence

Illustrated by
Dawn Cooper

WELBECK
CHILDREN'S BOOKS

Contents

Rules of the Forest

Respect the wildlife of the forest, whether they are animals, plants, fungi, birds, or insects.

Don't pick up anything unless you can identify it and have a grown-up present.

Keep to established paths.

Wear light-colored clothes so you can easily see ticks or other creatures that may land on you.

Don't make unnecessary noise.

Leave the forest as you found it, and take any trash home with you.

Health and safety for apprentice witches: Never touch or consume a plant unless you are absolutely certain of its identification. Use reference books to identify them. Always ask a grown-up to supervise when making the crafts and spells in this book.

Welcome

to the enchanted world of forests and the magical plants that grow within them!

The woodlands of the world are ancient and mysterious. They might be dark and dense pine forests or groves of beech trees, filled with dappled sunlight and smooth-barked trunks. Rainforests can be hot, tropical, and steamy, echoing with the cries of monkeys and bright-colored birds, or they may be mossy, cool, and silent, hidden by clouds of dripping mist. You will learn the secrets of trees and forests, the folk stories we tell about them, and the ways we use them in food, shelter, medicine . . . and magic.

You will discover specific forest-dwelling plants and the ways they have been used in spells and remedies – but beware: You must also understand which trees, leaves, nuts, and berries are safe and what each may be used for.

You will study woodland plants with magical qualities and the ways people have lived alongside forests through the centuries. You will learn about Ogham, the ancient tree alphabet, explore traditional customs and legends, find out how to create a protective amulet, and even discover how to use leaves to predict the future.

Good luck,

Madame Volare

The Forests of the World

There are lots of forests in the world, and magic may be found in all of them. Many are believed to be inhabited by gods, ghosts, goblins, and demons.

Tropical rainforests are hot and steamy all year round and are generally found within 10 degrees north and south of the equator. Gigantic trees form a top layer called a "canopy" many feet above the ground, which supports an entire ecosystem of plants, animals, and fungi.

According to Iquitos legend, the **Mayantu** is a strange creature of the Peruvian part of the Amazon rainforest. It looks like a goblin, but with the head of a frog, and it lives in at the top of **kapok** (*Ceiba pentandra*) trees. The Mayantu will help humans in trouble, but only if they have good intentions toward the forest.

Broadleaf forests are found in "temperate" regions that have mild temperatures and warm and cold seasons. They have mainly **deciduous** trees, which lose their leaves in the wintertime.

Foloï oak (*Quercus frainetto*) forest in Greece is named after **Pholus**, a half-human, half-horse centaur of Greek mythology.

Bamboo (*Bambusa vulgaris*) forests can be found in both tropical and mountainous regions, ranging from Africa and Asia to Central and South America.

In central Nepal, the shadow of the bamboo is said to invite death to a family, so it should be harvested only after dark.

Temperate rainforests are cool, wet woodlands that get a lot of rain and are often encased in clouds and fog.

The Great Bear Rainforest of British Columbia in Canada is home to the elusive **Spirit Bear**, which local Kitasoo / Xai'xais people believe has supernatural powers. Legend says that **Raven**, the creator god, gave one in every ten black bears white fur to remind humans of the time when the land was covered in snow. These Kermode bears, often born to regular black bear families, are very rare.

Yew (*Taxus baccata*) forests are rare, filled with gnarled, twisted **evergreens**. Bronze Age Celtic peoples believed yews to be symbols of eternal life, because they could sprout green leaves from seemingly dead wood.

The yew forest at **Kingley Vale** in the English South Downs is said to be a memorial to four Vikings after a great battle. The mounds on the top of the Downs are actually much older, but that doesn't stop the stories of Viking ghosts from haunting the woods. Even the trees are rumored to walk around at night!

Coniferous forests, which are usually made up of **evergreen**, cone-bearing trees, cover high places and mountainsides, including Northern Europe and North America. They are dense and dark, and said to be inhabited by many spirits.

According to Finnish mythology, the spirit **Tapio** rules the **pine** (*Pinus*) forests of Finland. His wife **Mielikki** heals the paws of creatures who have become caught in traps.

Practical Magic: A Spell Jar

Spell jars are small, lidded vessels containing objects that represent a spell caster's dreams, wishes, and intentions. Here's how to make one.

Find your jar. This can be any container with a secure lid—perhaps an old coffee or jam jar, or an interesting bottle, though it will work best if it has a wide neck.

Wash the jar thoroughly, then **decorate** it in whichever way you choose. You might paint it or glue interesting things to the outside. Buttons, ribbons, sequins, acorns, leaves, seeds—this is your spell jar, so go wild!

Spell jars are particularly powerful when you know what you want from them. Spend some time thinking about what you would like in life, so that you can channel your wishes into the jar. Things that people often wish for can include money, family, wellness, and friendship.

Find small items to represent your wish, and offer them to the jar. A coin might represent money, or a flower could stand in for a loved one. Try writing down a specific wish and add that, too. Embellish your spell with crystals, beads, feathers. Say your wishes as you fill your jar.

Seal the jar. Again, use anything you'd like—string, ribbon, glue, and tape will all work well.

Place it somewhere special. You could bury it in the yard, hide it in a closet, or even make a little altar (a personal space to keep special items) to display it, to remind you of your hopes and wishes.

Parts of a Tree

It's important to be able to identify the parts of a tree, so you know which are useful for each spell, charm, or other magical purpose.

Flower

Flowers protect trees' reproductive organs and attract pollinating insects. They often appear as masses of blossoms in springtime.

Cherry (*Prunus serrulata*) blossoms normally appear in mid-springtime, but an old Czech custom sees people bring a few bare cherry branches indoors in late November. Put them in water, and watch the almost-invisible buds miraculously burst into bloom in time for the winter solstice!

Canopy

The canopy or crown is a tree's outer layer of leaves, which receives most sunlight and rain. Anything growing below it will have reduced light and moisture.

In Polynesia, instead of "'Once upon a time," people start a tale with "Under the banyan tree," remembering long ago when storytellers would talk in the shade of the **banyan's** magnificent canopy.

Leaves

Leaves convert sunlight to energy via a process called photosynthesis.

A traditional magic spell involves writing a secret wish on a **bay** (*Laurus nobilis*) leaf, then either burning it or keeping it in your spell jar to add to the magic.

Fruit

Depending on variety, most trees bear fruit or nuts, which protect the seed.

Walnut (*Juglans*) husks are full of natural pigments and have been used to make inks and dyes for centuries. Walnut trees usually produce a rich brown but can change color if other plants or chemicals are added.

Trunk

A trunk is the tree's equivalent of a flower's stem. It channels water and nutrients between the roots and leaves, holds the tree upright, and raises the canopy to where it can get most light. Trunks are tough and strong, and they are often harvested for their wood.

Bark

Bark is the protective covering for the tree's trunk and has been used in medicine and magic for centuries.

Silver birch (*Betula pendula*), **eucalyptus** (*Eucalyptus*), and **paperbark maple** (*Acer griseum*) all naturally shed their bark. The peeling shreds can be collected and used instead of paper.

Branches

Branches project from the trunk in many directions, distributing water and nutrients to the leaves and supporting the canopy.

Traditionally, witches' broomstick handles are made from **ash** (*Fraxinus*) branches.

Wands made from **holly** (*Ilex*) twigs are said to banish unwelcome spirits.

Sap

Sap is a tree's lifeblood, a nutrient-filled fluid flowing around the tree. It's harvested as resin and used for anything from car tires to chewing gum!

Roots

Roots anchor a tree into the ground. They also absorb water and nutrients from the soil.

Because trees are so tall, roots often delve very deep, but they can also spread wide and shallow, depending on the type of earth.

In some parts of India, it is said that the roots of the **banyan** (*Ficus benghalensis*) grow forever, eventually reaching right through the earth.

In German folklore, some say that the Devil uses the roots of the **mulberry** (*Morus*) tree to shine his boots.

Walking sticks are traditionally made from the knobbly root of **blackthorn** (*Prunus spinosa*) that has been "coppiced," which means that it is carefully harvested each year to grow back as young wood.

Leaves

Identifying trees by their leaves is an important skill. They come in many sizes, shapes and forms, but most fit into a few specific types.

Coniferous trees have tiny, pointed leaves covered in a waxy substance that can stand the cold. These "needles" make up for their lack of size by staying on the tree, making energy all year, hence the name "**evergreen**." **Pine** (*Pinus*) needles can be soft or sharp, but often have a strong aroma. An old Scottish belief holds that sleeping on a pillow made of pine needles will cure catarrh (a buildup of mucus in the airways).

Deciduous trees tend to have broad leaves that make lots of energy in summertime. The leaves lose color and fall each autumn to preserve energy inside the plant through the winter. These trees come in many forms, and when they appear together, they are known as a "broadleaf" forest. Here are some of the forms they take:

Simple leaves are a single leaf attached to a stem. They can be any shape, with jagged, rounded, or smooth edges.

Oak (*Quercus*), **maple** (*Acer*), and **holly** (*Ilex*) are all examples of simple leaves.

In Japan, the fiery fall leaves of the **maple** (*Acer palmatum*) inspire people to dress in their best clothes for the tradition of Momijigari, or "red-leaf hunting."

Compound leaves

Compound leaves are two or more small "leaflets" attached to a single stem. They can also be lots of shapes, and sizes.

Palmately compound leaves have several leaflets all radiating from the same spot on the stem.

Horse chestnut (*Aesculus hippocastanum*) is a typical example of palmately compound leaves. Some people say that it gets its name from the horseshoe-shaped scar left on the stem by the leaf when it falls.

Pinnately compound leaves are small pairs of leaves growing from a central stem. **Elder** (*Sambucus nigra*), **rowan** (*Sorbus*), and **ash** (*Fraxinus*) all have pinnate leaves.

Most **ash** (*Fraxinus*) leaves have a series of pairs of leaves, with a single leaf at the end. In parts of England, if you can find one with just the pairs of leaves and no single leaf, you can make a wish.

Bipinnately compound leaves are complex. They not only have small leaves growing from a central stem, but each of the leaves is also a little stem, which has even smaller leaves growing from it!

The **Persian silk** (*Albizia julibrissin*) tree has bipinnate leaves. In China, it is called He-Huan—the tree of happiness. It folds up its leaves each night, which is possibly why it is used to treat insomnia (the inability to sleep).

Nuts

While some trees such as **apple** (*Malus*) and **peach** (*Prunus persica*) bear soft fruit, some fruits have a hard protective shell and are called nuts. They have many magical stories and uses, but are almost always associated with wealth and abundance.

The ancient Romans associated **walnuts** (*Juglans*) with Jupiter, the king of the gods.

Some people eat a few **almonds** (*Prunus dulcis*) before important meetings to ensure a good outcome.

Brazil nuts (*Bertholletia excelsa*) cannot be farmed, they have to be gathered from the floor of the Amazon rainforest by *castañeros* (harvesters).

Pecan (*Carya illinoinensis*) comes from a First Nations Algonquin word for "a nut that must be cracked with a stone."

A Filipino legend tells how a fairy granted the **cashew's** (*Anacardium occidentale*) wish to look outside its dark case, so it could watch the animals having a party. It has been peeking outside its shell ever since!

In Parsi and Hindu traditions, a **coconut** (*Cocos nucifera*) is broken over the doorway of newlyweds to bring good luck.

Chinese people give gifts of **pistachios** (*Pistacia vera*) during Chinese New Year to bring happiness and wealth through the coming months.

Practical Magic: Grow a Pine Tree for Prosperity

There are more than 800 varieties of pine (*Pinus*) tree. Not all "pine nuts" are edible, but if you can find a fresh pine cone before the squirrels do, and if it is still closed, you can grow a pine tree to bring good luck. Here's how to grow one:

Don't plant your pine seeds yet. Put the cone in the freezer for three months to trick the seeds into thinking it's wintertime.

After three months, take the pine cone out of the freezer. You will still need to be patient since it often takes several weeks for the tightly closed cone to open and reveal its seeds.

Sow the seeds in a small tray of gritty soil, place in a sunny position outdoors, and keep it damp (not wet).

According to tradition, you and your family will prosper as the tree germinates and grows.

The Forest in Spring and Summer

At the start of spring, deciduous tree branches are bare, and the forest floor is dark with fallen leaves. But those empty branches are changing color. Tiny knobbles are growing under the bark, giving the tree a dark, reddish-purple hue. Deep inside, sap is slowly warming in the weak sunlight and rising up through the trunk, filling the branches and swelling once-invisible buds with life.

Sap can be tasty for humans, too. In the United States and Canada, people score lines into sugar maple (*Acer saccharum*) trees and hang buckets around them to collect the maple syrup.

One of the first trees to come into leaf in the spring is the **silver birch** (*Betula pendula*). Birch brooms (besoms) are used in many European countries to sweep the house, ready for spring. Perhaps this is why the shape of the first letter of the **ogham** alphabet (made up of different symbols) is of a birch tree.

The **Japanese plum** called ume (*Prunus salicina*) usually bursts into sweet-smelling flowers in early February. People are so excited to see it, they dress up for Shobai, a plum festival. Later, they will also enjoy Hanami, where they seek out cherry blossoms.

By midsummer, the forest is fully clothed in bright-green leaves. The **bracken** (*Pteridium*) is waist-high, so fewer flowering plants can find enough light to grow. **Foxgloves** (*Digitalis*) are tall enough to capture the dappled sunlight of a woodland glade, along with little **herb Robert** (*Geranium robertianum*). Wear a sprig in your buttonhole for good luck.

Oak (*Quercus*) is one of the most esteemed trees in mythology, and it is so important to nature. A single oak tree is its own ecosystem, supporting more life than any other tree. Up to 200 species rely on it, including bats and squirrels, beetles and fungi, and humans celebrate it, too. In ancient times, people touched a "fairy door" in the oak to cure diseases. We now know that the "door" is the swelling where a branch has fallen off, but it is still magical to find one.

If you stand beneath the "quaking tree" or **aspen** (*Populus tremuloides*), you may hear a magical message as its silver-backed leaves rustle in the breeze. The tree has always been thought of as a communicator between this world and the spirit one.

In 16th and 17th century Germany, tanzlinde were literally "dancing **limes**" (*Tilia*). Young people would dance below the lime trees, while an orchestra sat in the branches and played above them.

Magical Flowers of the Forest Floor

Because the forest becomes so dense in the summer, most temperate woodland flowers are found in spring. The tropical rainforest enjoys year-round leaf cover, so the flowers there have adapted to low light levels.

There are thousands of varieties in the **orchid** (Orchidaceae) family, found all over the world except the North and South Poles. The earliest cultivated orchids were **boat orchids** (*Cymbidium*), much-prized in China because they symbolize purity and friendship.

Each spring, **bluebells** (*Hyacinthoides non-scripta*) fill English woodlands with a carpet of blue. They were once associated with witches' potions, and some said that anyone who wandered into a bluebell grove would fall under the spell of the fairies. Beware: All parts of the bluebell are poisonous.

Sweet violets (*Viola odorata*) are often called "shrinking" or "shy" plants because they hide in the darker parts of a wood or hedgerow. They have a beautiful scent, so are a traditional part of bridal bouquets. If you wear a sprig in your buttonhole, take it off before you go indoors, and leave it for the fairies.

Heliconia (*Heliconia psittacorum*) is also known as, including "lobster claw," and "toucan's beak." It blooms across the Amazon rainforest. The Maroon people of Suriname use it as a protective charm.

The cacao tree (*Theobroma cacao*) may have strange-looking pink pods hanging from its sparsely leaved branches, but looks aren't everything—in Latin, *theobroma* means "food of the gods." The ancient Mesoamerican people believed their gods discovered the plant and gave it to humans.

The tiny white stars of **wood anemones** (*Anemone nemorosa*) are traditionally considered unlucky. Perhaps this is because the flower is poisonous—the Chinese call it "the flower of death"—so never touch it!

The spooky white **ghost pipe** (*Monotropa uniflora*) does not contain **chorophyll** and does not **photosynthesize**, so it can live in some of North America's darkest forests. According to Cherokee legend, the plant grows where friends have quarreled.

The Forest in Fall and Winter

As the year turns, the inhabitants of the forest begin to think about winter. Many animals, from bears to hedgehogs, hibernate. Trees do the same. The leaves of deciduous trees can't withstand winter's cold temperatures, so they must be shed. Any remaining nutrients return to the tree, losing their green chlorophyll and leaving only their true colors: yellow, orange, red, brown. The leaves then fall, in a process called abscission.

Few plants can grow in **beech** (*Fagus*) woods because the roots grow in dense mats near the surface, but one mysterious organism loves this tough environment. A fungus called *Tuber aestivum* grows under or nearby the roots, creating sweet-smelling truffles. Both the fungus and the tree gain nutrients from the deal in what is called a **symbiotic** relationship. Humans like to eat truffles, but they are hard to find, so even today we train pigs and dogs to sniff them out.

The winged fruits or "samara" of the **sycamore** (*Acer pseudoplatanus*) flutter gently to the ground, protecting the seeds. It is the tree of **Freya**, Norse goddess of love and war. Gather some for your spell jar to represent harmony and energy.

Apple (*Malus*) is often associated with the Celtic festival of **Samhain**, which marks the end of summer. It is said that the veil between the worlds of humans and spirits is very thin at this time, and apples are still a part of Halloween **divination** games.

Winter sees the last of the deciduous trees stripped to bare branches, but they will survive in the cold and frost. There is still color, however, for now is the time of the evergreen.

Pine (*Pinus*) forests are often the settings for folk tales, some frightening, others sweet. Baba Yaga, the witch of Slavic folklore, is said to live among the pines in a house on chicken legs, surrounded by a fence of bones and skulls. She is sometimes evil, sometimes kind, as is her forest.

The glossy, prickly **holly** (*Ilex*) has always been a favorite at Christmas, especially while it still bears its red berries; but don't bring it into the house too soon, because according to Welsh legend it can lead to arguments. Christmas Eve is considered the best time to bring holly indoors, though it may be safely used during Advent for church decorations.

Ivy (*Hedera*) is not a tree, but it can cover other trees so much that it looks like one. Like holly, you should be careful not to bring ivy into the house too soon, since in some parts of Britain, even a piece brought in by accident can attract bad luck!

Enter the Magical Forest

The path seems welcoming, the forest beckons, but approach with care. Nearly all woods are very old indeed, and the trees within them have lived for longer than many generations of humans.

Trees are the lifeblood of the forest. Plants grow at their roots, birds live in their branches, insects buzz around their trunks, and animals shelter in their hollows. Even the fungi spreading underground enjoy a special relationship with trees.

There is magic in the woods, ingredients for spells, inspiration for meditation, and moments of calm for the mind and body. But remember, you may only gather items that the tree has shed—acorns, ash helicopters, autumn leaves, and fallen twigs—do nothing that will hurt the forest or disturb the creatures and forest folk that live here. Every tree is believed to be protected by some spirit or deity, and as legend will tell you, terrible things happen to the people who inflict harm to the trees.

You will learn more about how people have channeled the magic of trees in the following pages, and how many—like the elder, oak, and rowan—will protect those who revere them.

The World Tree

The idea of the "axis mundi"—that there is a line through the center of the world connecting the earth with the heavens—is thousands of years old. In many cultures, this line takes the form of a sprawling tree.

Often, the gods live in the highest branches, humans inhabit the area around the trunk, and the dark lords of the underworld dwell in its roots. Various creatures live there, too, such as the brightly colored **Simurgh**, which resembles a phoenix and inhabits the branches of the ancient Persian world tree. Beasts lurk among the roots, such as malevolent dragons and, sometimes, terrifying sea monsters.

The **Bai-Terek** of the Turkic peoples from Eastern Europe and Asia, is a golden **poplar** (*Populus*) tree. The two-headed eagle that lives at the top is constantly on the lookout for **Erlik**, god of death, who, in the form of a snake, keeps slithering up the trunk to steal its eggs.

Yggdrasil, the Norse world for tree, is an **ash** (*Fraxinus*). **Nidhogg** the dragon lurks in the underworld, gnawing at the tree's roots. Even though he has never met the eagle that lives in the topmost branches, they are deadly enemies because naughty **Ratatoskr**, the squirrel, runs up and down the trunk conveying rude messages between them.

Other animals are less threatening: **Fusang**, the ancient Chinese spirit tree, is a mulberry (*Morus*) that is home to a roost of celestial chickens who wake up the world's poultry every morning.

Ogham

Archaeologists have found around 400 examples of Ogham (pronounced "oh-am"), an alphabet used to write early Irish and sometimes western British languages. It looks like runes, another ancient writing system from northern Europe, but it is not the same. Ogham is based on native trees so is sometimes known as the Celtic tree alphabet.

No one knows how old Ogham is, but scripts written with it date back to at least the fourth century. Scholars are still figuring out exactly how it worked, but each letter, called a *feda*, has a central line like a tree trunk and uses different *nin* (branches) to represent a specific tree. They may also have been finger signs so people could communicate via secret hand signals.

Some of Ogham's "alphabet" trees have been identified, but others are still only guesses. Perhaps you will eventually decipher the rest of the meanings!

Beith—birch (*Betula*)

Feàrn—alder (*Alnus*)

Saille—willow (*Salix*)

Duir—oak (*Quercus*)

Coll—hazel (*Corylus*)

Iogh—yew (*Taxus*)

Warning!—Raw rowan berries contain parasorbic acid, which can cause indigestion and sometimes kidney damage, so never eat them without cooking them first. Once they are cooked, the parasorbic acid converts into sorbic acid, which is harmless.

Magical Tree: Rowan
(Sorbus)

Clinging to rocky crags and freezing mountainsides in the northernmost parts of Europe, **rowan** is one of the most magical of all trees.

Rowan has been associated with protection ever since Thor, Norse god of thunder, was saved by a branch that dipped into the fast-flowing river he had fallen into. For centuries, sailors ensured that their ships contained at least one plank of rowan wood. They were careful where they got it from, though, because rowan also protected the graves of wrongfully executed people, and if one of those trees was felled, the ship would sink.

In Celtic mythology, rowan was sacred to Brid, goddess of the arts, healing, and weaving, so spindles and spinning wheels were often made from it.

Every rowan berry comes with its own magical symbol: a five-pointed star or "pentagram" in its base. We now know that this is where the flower has died away, but the sign has always been thought of as lucky, and rowan sprigs were used to protect everything from cattle sheds to babies' cradles.

Even today, it is considered very lucky to plant a rowan and, especially in Scotland, extremely unlucky to chop one down.

Practical Magic: A Rowan Amulet

Sticks of rowan were traditionally kept in cottage corners to repel bad spirits and over hearths to ensure fires lit properly; but it was also worn as a charm to protect someone or something from evil. Rowan amulets were especially popular with sailors and fishermen to safeguard them during storms.

How to Make Your Amulet

You will need:

Some soft twigs and leaves from a rowan tree
A little red thread, which is associated with safety
Some ribbon, any color and long enough to hang up your amulet.

Gently work the twigs into a small loop or cross. Circles are especially popular, even though no one can quite remember why evil cannot pass through one!

Tie securely with red thread, and hang your amulet from the ribbon.

Decide how you would like to show off your amulet. Traditionally, they protect the home, so you could hang it in your bedroom. But if it's very small, you could wear it around your neck.

Magical Tree: Oak
(Quercus)

The majestic oak is associated with wisdom, sacred to some of the most important gods in world mythology. It was much loved by the druids, priests, magicians, and soothsayers of the ancient Celtic religion.

Oaks have been considered very powerful in European and especially British folklore, representing both good and evil, depending on how people treated them.

Anyone who disrespected an oak tree was punished in terrible ways. Someone who felled an oak might lose an eye or even drop dead as a massive branch fell on top of them.

If you can find an "oak apple"—a small, round **gall** made by a tiny wasp—on Michaelmas Day (September 29) you may see the future by opening it. According to an old English superstition, if you find a little worm, it will be a good year. A fly suggests the next twelve months will be moderately good—but woe betide anyone who finds a spider inside!

The oak rewarded respect with protection, famously hiding the fugitive English Prince Charles from the Parliamentarian army. The day that he returned as King Charles II became known as Oak Apple Day, when people wore sprigs of oak in celebration. Anyone not wearing an oak leaf could be pelted with eggs, stung with nettles, or pinched.

A Woodland Wheel to Channel Positivity

The sacred circle is a traditional symbol representing the continuous cycle of life. Each culture uses the symbol differently, including for medicine or to find an individual's inner power.

You Will Need:
A selection of small objects freely "given" by the forest—not picked or dug up.

These might include twigs, leaves, feathers, snail shells, stones, bark, seedcases, nuts, flowers, and berries. Just make sure that you don't pick up anything you can't identify as safe to handle.

Lay the gathered objects on the woodland floor, in a circle large enough for you to sit or stand inside.

Go inside your circle, and use the energy of the wheel to concentrate on the natural world. Listen to birds and the rustle of the wind in the trees, smell the earth, and see the sights around you.

Spend as long as you need in the stillness, noticing how everything is connected.

When you are ready to leave, make sure that anything you leave behind will disappear back into the forest, honoring the positive energy that nature has given you.

The Enchanted Forest

The glade is beautiful, silent, and deserted. Or is it? There is enchantment here. Forest spirits may be good or evil, often depending on how respectful humans are to the woodland.

Kodama are the spirits of Japan's most ancient trees, which sometimes wander the forests as faint orbs of light or tiny, blobby human shapes. They bless the homes of people who honor them, but they die if their tree is cut down, taking any good fortune with them.

Dryads are woodland nymphs of ancient Greek mythology. Some dryads care for a single tree while others look after a whole species. Morea, who guards mulberry trees, was so important she is remembered in its scientific name, *Morus*.

The Nang Tani haunts groves of wild banana (*Musa acuminata*) trees in Thailand. She punishes men who have been cruel to women but is generous to anyone who is kind and considerate.

In northern European folklore, **Goblins** are usually mischievous rather than outright evil. **Puck**, also known as Robin Goodfellow, is a trickster hobgoblin from Celtic legend. He mainly plays pranks on both humans and fairies but occasionally does good deeds.

The **Erlking** is the dark king of the elves. He is considered very dangerous—some stories say he can kill with a single touch of his frosty finger.

Most **trolls**, the dangerous giants of Norse folklore, mainly live in rocks and mountains. Keep a careful lookout, though, for the forest-dwelling variety, who will uproot entire trees to use as weapons. Luckily, they're usually very stupid and are easily tricked!

Beware, too, the **Skogsrå**, Swedish Mistress of the Forest. She can seem very nice and is often beautiful—from the waist up. Her lower half, however, may be a rotting tree trunk or have cows' hooves and a tail. Anyone who follows her into the woods may never be seen again.

Trees of the Gods

Many trees are associated with gods of different faiths, both ancient and modern. Some trees are sacred to several gods!

In ancient Greek mythology, the myrtle (*Myrtus*) was sacred to Aphrodite, goddess of love. Perhaps this is why it became a lucky plant for a bride to include in her wedding bouquet.

Konohanasakuya-hime (conn-o-hanna-sack-ooyar-hi-may) is the Japanese goddess of volcanoes, also known as the Blossom Princess because her flower is the sakura (cherry blossom, *Prunus serrulata*). Her flowers are beautiful but die quickly, a reminder that life is wonderful but short and should be enjoyed.

In the medieval Welsh poem "Cad Goddeu," Gywdion, the trickster god of magic and poetry, enchants the trees of the forest to fight as his army. It is said Gwydion made his wands from ash (*Fraxinus*) branches.

In Hindu tradition, the fragrant sandalwood (*Santalum album*) is sacred to the great god Shiva the Destroyer, though some believe it is also a favorite of Vishnu the Preserver.

Freya and Venus, goddesses of love in Norse and Roman mythologies, both reign over the linden (*Tilia*) and have given the tree their blessing: heart-shaped leaves that whisper of romance.

Osiris, the ancient Egyptian god of the afterlife, is often depicted with a staff of intertwined serpents topped by a pine cone, symbolizing the all-seeing eye.

A legend of the Southern African San people tells how the sky god Kaang threw the baobab (*Adansonia*) tree out of his heavenly garden. It landed upside down on Earth and grew where it was, which is why it looks today as though its roots are in the air.

According to a Canadian First Nations Salteaux folktale, the famous trickster god Nanabozho was very grateful to the maple (*Acer*) tree for sheltering his grandmother, so he caused its sap to run sweet—then he taught humans how to tap it! Never trust a trickster god . . .

The twisted juniper (*Juniperus*) is sacred to Asherah, the ancient mother goddess. Archaeologists recently found a 7,500-year-old juniper stump believed to be the oldest representation of Asherah in the world.

Holly (*Ilex*) is sacred to Thor and Taranis, gods of thunder to the Norse folk and the Celts. It is unlucky to cut the tree, so they often poke up above the line of a hedge. This serves another purpose: It stops witches from dancing along the top!

Magical Tree: Hawthorn

(Crataegus)

Crataegus is usually known as **hawthorn**, from the Old English *Hagedorn* or "hedge-thorn." It is used in hedges because it grows very fast, but, above all, it is the tree of the fairies. The "**Gentle Folk**" prefer to live in single hawthorns in the middle of fields, and bad luck will follow any farmer that cuts one down. But if humans hang a branch of it over their cattle shed door, the fairies will protect the cows inside.

Before the Gregorian calendar came into effect, hawthorn used to bloom in May. People would go "a-maying" in the countryside viewing "May blossoms," playing pranks on each other, dancing, and singing. However, they never brought the flowers into the house because hawthorn is also one of the unluckiest flowers in Britain. One of its many other names is "mother-die," and some people say it smells of death.

Magical Tree: Hazel
(Corylus)

Pilgrims and warriors fashioned staffs from hazel, ideally cut on the Sabbath to ward off witches. Irish emigrants making their way to North America carried pieces of hazelwood in their pockets to ensure a safe journey.

Hazelnuts were often used on Nut-Crack Night (another word for Halloween), when they were used to play **divination** games. The next day, the local vicar had to put up with people cracking and noisily eating the leftover nuts in church!

Hazel is sacred to the Norse god **Thor**, the Roman god **Mercury**, his Greek equivalent **Hermes**, and in the Christian church, **St. Philibert**, because the nuts were said to begin to ripen on his saint's day, August 20. The nuts are still called "filberts" in some places.

Celtic legend tells of nine **hazel** trees that grew around a pool, dropping their nuts into the water. A salmon ate the nuts, making it the wisest creature on Earth. A druid caught the fish and instructed his apprentice to cook it for him. The apprentice did not eat any fish, but he did lick a splash of juice from his thumb, bringing him instant wisdom. He later became the Irish hero **Fionn Mac Cumhaill**, from *coll*, the Celtic word for hazel, making him "Finn, son of Hazel".

The Forest by Night

Everyone should experience the magic of visiting a forest after dark. With a few precautions, you will find a completely different world to the woodland you've seen by daylight.

VERY IMPORTANT: Never enter the forest alone—especially at night. There are many hazards out there in the dark, so always make sure you have a trusted adult with you.

Wear plenty of warm clothing. The forest gets very cold after sunset.

Bring a flashlight, but DO NOT USE IT except in an emergency, or you will miss the best parts and may startle nocturnal creatures.

Allow your eyes to adjust to the light. You will be surprised how quickly you will start to see amazing things in what was inky blackness. That white swirl of stars is the Milky Way, our home galaxy. The ancient Polynesians thought it was a great celestial shark that feasted on clouds.

If you are exploring the forest during the full moon, you will have plenty of light, but some superstitions consider it an "unstable" time, filled with unwanted energies! Take special care . . .

Use your senses—your eyes may be less useful than your ears, nose, and the feel of things under your feet and outstretched fingers.

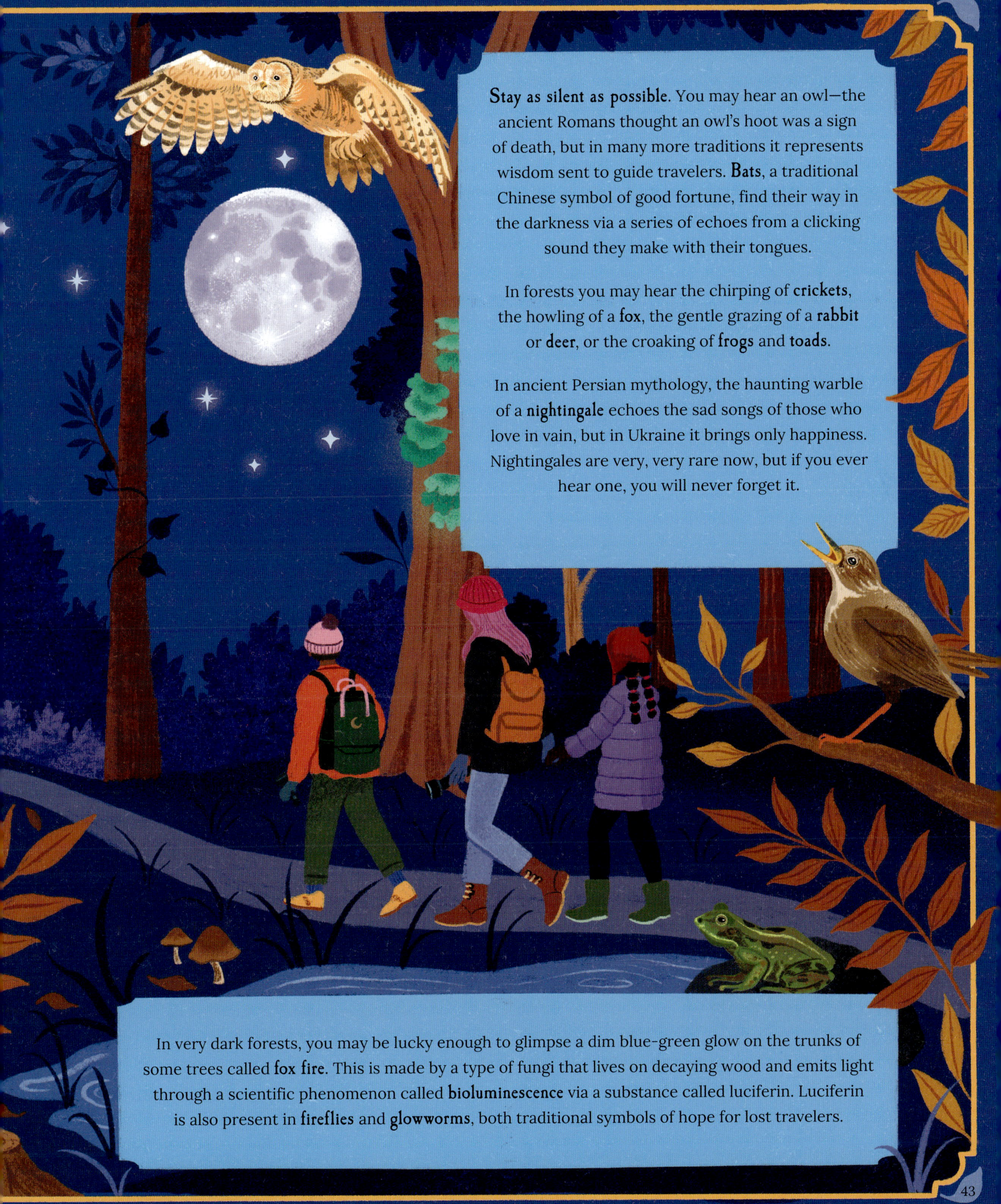

Stay as silent as possible. You may hear an owl—the ancient Romans thought an owl's hoot was a sign of death, but in many more traditions it represents wisdom sent to guide travelers. **Bats**, a traditional Chinese symbol of good fortune, find their way in the darkness via a series of echoes from a clicking sound they make with their tongues.

In forests you may hear the chirping of **crickets**, the howling of a **fox**, the gentle grazing of a **rabbit** or **deer**, or the croaking of **frogs** and **toads**.

In ancient Persian mythology, the haunting warble of a **nightingale** echoes the sad songs of those who love in vain, but in Ukraine it brings only happiness. Nightingales are very, very rare now, but if you ever hear one, you will never forget it.

In very dark forests, you may be lucky enough to glimpse a dim blue-green glow on the trunks of some trees called **fox fire**. This is made by a type of fungi that lives on decaying wood and emits light through a scientific phenomenon called **bioluminescence** via a substance called luciferin. Luciferin is also present in **fireflies** and **glowworms**, both traditional symbols of hope for lost travelers.

Lightning Trees

What is that weird tree standing alone at the top of the hill? Its branches are jagged and broken, and when you get closer, it becomes clear that it has been hit by some strange force . . .

Today we know that lightning is an enormous electrical spark crashing to the ground with a gigantic flash of light and a deafening noise. It is completely natural, but in the past people thought it was a sign that they had angered the gods. Virtually every faith had a god of thunder and lightning, from the Norse **Thor** and Greek **Zeus**, to the Hindu **Indra**, **Xolotl** of the Aztecs, and **Oya**, the Nigerian Yoruba goddess of storms.

Trees seem to attract lightning, but this is usually because the energy is looking for the shortest way to get to the ground, and trees are the tallest things around. The tiny prickles of **holly** (*Ilex*) leaves are said to act like tiny lightning conductors, so people sometimes plant a holly tree next to their homes for protection.

People also once protected themselves by making amulets and charms from "thunderstruck" wood. This may derive from a widespread belief that lightning never strikes the same place twice.

First Nation Cherokee people believed that storm-struck trees absorbed lightning's energy, making them sacred. A struck tree that was still alive was even more powerful, since the energy still coursed through it, which also made it very dangerous. Only specially trained medicine people were allowed to use such hazardous magic.

In some parts of Wales, the idea of a hollow "blasted oak" can be unlucky. Be careful if you look inside: It may be hiding unknown horrors!

Not all hollow trees are made by lightning. Some are the product of "heartwood fungi"—a type of mushroom that eats dead wood cells from inside. This does not necessarily kill the tree—in fact, it helps to clear bad stuff from the center and provides habitats for wildlife.

Forest Folk

Originally the word *forest* meant land set aside for hunting. It almost always belonged to a king, and regular folk were not allowed. Those who dared to live there were treated with suspicion and often fear.

The **Gamekeeper** was employed to stop people from stealing food or fuel from the forest. He was usually very unpopular. The Elizabethan ghost of **Herne the Hunter** wears stag's antlers and is thought to rattle chains on dark nights in Windsor Great Park, England.

Poachers were people driven to stealing forest animals for food. In Lancashire, England, they tell of two poachers who heard the stolen animals in their sacks talking. Realizing that they'd accidentally caught two fairies, they ran away. The next day, their empty sacks were found neatly folded by the side of the road.

Charcoal burners lived alone in the forest, baking wood for people's fires, but the townsfolk feared them. What else did they get up to in the wild wood? Drinking? Magic? Murder...? Some said they kept serpents as pets, though in reality the snakes attracted to the warmth would have been dangerous to the burners.

Outlaws lived in hiding to escape punishment for breaking the law. It is unlikely that **Robin Hood** ever existed, but the medieval outlaw **Roger Godberd** really did live in Sherwood Forest with a band of men and really did steal from the rich. He just forgot to give it to the poor!

Fortune-Telling through Trees

Divination is an art not easily mastered, and everyone must find their own best medium for "scrying" (peeping) into the magical realm. Through the ages, many kinds of trees and many parts of trees have been used to receive important messages, revelations, and guidance.

Sycomancy, from the Greek word *Sýko*, meaning "**fig**," is the art of divination through fig leaves. Write a question on a fig leaf—the longer the ink takes to dry, the more positive the answer will be.

A very strange old English custom saw people write their names on **ivy** leaves (*Hedera*) on either Halloween or Twelfth Night. They dropped the leaves into water. By the next morning, if any of the names had changed into images of coffins, they would die soon!

Tasseomancy involves the questioner drinking a cup of tea brewed with loose leaves, then turning the nearly empty cup upside down in the saucer. The scryer interprets the shapes left by the tea leaves. Popular across Europe, it is particularly associated with Romany people. In Turkey and the Middle East, a similar form is practiced using coffee grounds. In Victorian times, "reading tea leaves" was such a popular pastime that special cups and saucers were made with interpretations printed on them!

Magical Tree: Yew
(*Taxus*)

WARNING:
Always exercise caution around yew trees, and avoid touching or ingesting any part of them.

Dark, shadowy, and silent, the **yew** (*Taxus baccata*) is one of the most mysterious plants on Earth. It constantly replenishes itself and is even a Celtic symbol of eternal life, but no one knows how old any individual tree may be. Some people guess, but there is no way of finding the exact truth. We can't use normal methods of dating a tree—**dendrochronology** (counting the rings) or the scientific method known as **carbon-14**—because very ancient yews become hollow, so there is nothing to test!

Yew has been grown at the gates of graveyards since Roman times, when it was sacred to **Hecate**, goddess of entranceways, witchcraft, and the moon. It is still often found in churchyards. Some people think that this means that churches are built on old temple sites. Others say that they are just the lucky survivors from when entire yew forests were cut down to make longbows in the Middle Ages.

Every part of the yew is poisonous, which may be why it is often associated with death. One strange old belief told that the roots thrive on dead bodies. Another legend said that of course that was nonsense—the tree only soaked up noxious juices emitted by the corpse!

The Haunted Forest

The forest is dark and still, the shadows loom.
What's lurking in the wild wood? Phantoms? Demons?
Who knows—perhaps a whole host of spirits may
come thundering through the darkness . . .

The **Wild Hunt** is one of the most common European woodland motifs. Depending on which country you are in, this ghostly party chases through forests as the "furious army," "terrifying ride," or the "green huntsmen." Its leader may be the Norse god **Odin**, the Norwegian witch **Guro Rysserova**, **King Arthur** of Britain, **Gronveld** the Danish huntsman, who rides with his head under his arm, or even the evil Catalonian **Comte Arnau**, condemned to ride for eternity, his flesh constantly devoured by flames. Humans should avert their eyes, lest they be trampled underfoot or accidentally caught up in the ride themselves.

Some ghosts have names, like poor **Amy Robsart**, first wife of Robert Dudley, Earl of Leicester, who mysteriously fell down the stairs to her death in 1560. Legend tells how she later appeared to her husband in the forest of Wychwood, Oxfordshire, England, and predicted his death ten days later.

Locals believe the Dow Hill Forest at Kurseong, near Darjeeling, is India's most haunted hill station. Woodcutters get the distinct feeling of being watched and sometimes hear footsteps, and there have been rare sightings of a headless young boy and a **woman in gray**.

New Jersey, USA, has its own demon, the **Jersey Devil**. Boasting wings, a goat's head and hooves, sightings have been made in the Pine Barrens forests for at least 250 years.

Yawata no Yabushirazu is just a very small woodland in Ichikawa, Japan, but it has become so notorious for people being **kamikakushi** ("spirited away") that the name has become associated with mazes or labyrinths. No one knows what the problem—have suggested the ghost of a **samurai** (warrior) or that there is a bottomless pit leaking poisonous gas. Others blame a mischievous **kitsune** (fox spirit).

A Real Ghost Tree

The mysterious **giant redwoods** (*Sequoiadendron giganteum*) in California can live for more than 2,000 years. Every so often, however, one appears that is entirely without colour. Until recently no one understood how these "ghost trees" could live, because they don't have **chlorophyll**. Some even accused them of being "vampires" that sucked the life out of the trees around them. Scientists noticed, however, that they often grow in places where there are dangerous toxins in the soil. They now think that the other trees may allow the "ghosts" to take nourishment from their roots, because they also suck up the poisons that would kill normal plants.

Parasites, Epiphytes, and Walking Trees

Not all the plants of the forest are trees, and not all trees are what they seem . . .

What's that strange scruffy "bird's nest" high up in that tree? **Witch's broom** is actually the tree's own twigs that have been confused into growing in weird directions by an infection from either an insect, bacteria, or fungus.

Parasites are organisms that get food from another "host" organism. Because the **ghost pipe** (*Monotropa uniflora*) feeds from its host, the **beech tree** (*Fagus*), it has no need for **chlorophyll**. Cherokee myth says its flowers are chiefs of various tribes, turned to ghosts by the Great Spirit after they quarreled over the peace pipe.

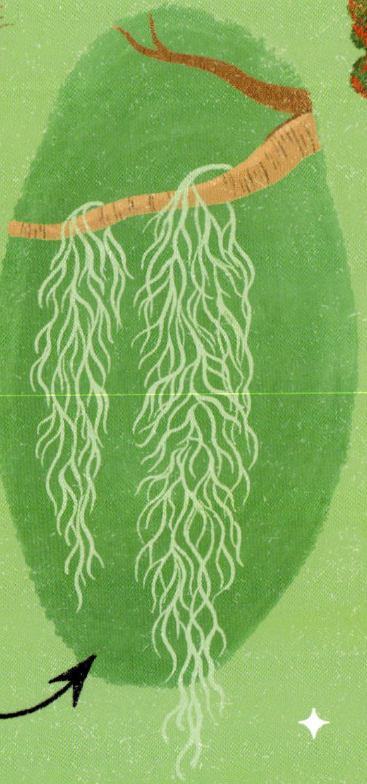

Trees in the Southern United States are often draped with spooky, spidery, spiky "hair" called **Spanish moss** (*Tillandsia usneoides*). Florida legend tells how the evil pirate Gorez Goz became entangled in the tree's branches. His scratchy beard has grown there ever since. Spanish moss is **epiphytic**—a plant that grows on another plant—it is not a parasite, it just lives there.

Not all epiphytes are so nice. The famous **rata** (*Metrosideros robusta*) of New Zealand starts out just growing on the **rimu** tree (*Dacrydium cupressinum*). As it gets older, its massive root system slowly encases its host. The rata still doesn't suck the tree's nutrients, but choked, the rimu dies anyway, leaving the rata, which can grow to over 82 feet tall. Maori people use nectar from its bright red flowers to treat sore throats.

Walking Trees

There are many legends of "walking" trees, often considered magical by the cultures that know them. But can it really be true? Can trees walk?

The three witches in Shakespeare's play *Macbeth* warn the ruthless Scottish king that he should fear for his crown when Birnam Wood moves to his stronghold at Dunsinane, Scotland. Macbeth thinks he is safe, until he sees the trees moving toward him in the form of an army camouflaged with branches from the forest. Just two of Birnam's trees remain today: an elderly **oak** (*Quercus*) and doddering **sycamore** (*Acer pseudoplatanus*).

Yew (*Taxus*) has a reputation for creeping slowly across the forest floor, though you will never see one walk. Over the centuries, they send out long branches that take root as they touch the ground, making a new part of the trunk and moving the tree a short distance.

No one agrees on how true the stories told about the enormous **walking palm** (*Socratea exorrhiza*) of South and Central American rainforests are. The bottom of its trunk splits into dozens of "stilt roots" just above the ground, which look like little legs, leading to tales of it wandering around the forest looking for the sun. This is not true, but as it replenishes its roots and old ones die, it does "move" a very short distance over many years.

The Forest Floor

However majestic trees may be, you must also understand the woodland realm at your feet.

mosses

Mosses are nonflowering plants that date back 450 million years. They live in cold, dark, damp places. In the northern hemisphere, lost travelers may find north by looking for the side of a tree trunk that has moss growing on it. In the southern hemisphere, the moss side indicates south.

Moss people are said to be tiny moss-covered folk that dwell in the forests of Bavaria, Germany. They are simple and kind, and any human kindness is always repaid many times over with good luck.

Leshy, a forest dweller from Slavic mythology, usually appears as a grumpy, elderly humanoid who hides behind fallen branches. He is often thought of as evil but if people treat the leshy's world with respect, he may grudgingly help them.

Bracken (*Pteridium aquilinum*) is one of the most common plants in the world. In parts of rural France, bracken was carried to protect against werewolves, witches, and evil spirits. In Russia, its fronds were waved to guard against being drowned by the Rusalka, a female spirit that lived in the pools and rivers of the forest.

The brightly colored **cuckoopint** (*Arum maculatum*) is as poisonous as it looks. It has tiny needles that produce a nasty rash, and it will make you extremely sick if you eat it, so don't touch it. The medieval herbalist Nicholas Culpeper thought it very useful, though. He mixed it with hot ox poop and put it on the legs of people suffering from gout!

In many folktales, gold given to travelers by fairies turns out to be nothing but dried leaves. According to these legends, then, the soil of the forest floor is mainly made of "**fairy gold**"! The leaves have been broken down by fungi, making lightweight "leaf mold."

The Magic of Mushrooms

Fungi are neither plants nor animals, but an entire kingdom by themselves. They have always been mysterious, and even today we don't understand everything about them.

WARNING:
You should never touch any mushroom unless you are with a fungi expert. Many deadly mushrooms look like edible ones, so while it is fine to look at them and learn about their lore, do not pick any.

Tremella mesenterica is one of a number of fungi known as **witches'-butter**. Often bright yellow, it can be found smeared up branches in woodlands. In Sweden, it was said to be splashes made by careless fairies churning magical butter.

Octopus stinkhorn (*Clathrus archeri*) looks like an alien from outer space! Its bright-pink tentacles "hatch" from strange, whitish "eggs," and it smells like rotting flesh. Perhaps this is why it is also called devil's fingers!

Death cap (*Amanita phalloides*) is one of the most poisonous mushrooms there is—Roman historians tell us that it killed Emperor Claudius. Although scientists are working on an antidote, it is still an extremely dangerous fungus, and when young it looks very much like a field mushroom. Do not touch.

Certain fungi send out tiny threads called **mycelium**, making vast underground networks between trees sometimes called the "wood wide web." This is not dangerous to the trees; in fact, it is thought that they and the fungi help each other. It may even be a way that trees can communicate with each other.

It is very bad luck to step into a mushroom **fairy ring**. You will be whisked away to dance with the "Gentle Folk" (fairies) and may never return.

In Hawaii, fairy rings are known as **Menehune** rings after the magical little people that build things at night. First Nations Americans suggest that the circles are left by dancing bison, while in Germany they are called **Hexenringe** after the witches that conjure them.

In Central Asia, storms are said to be caused by a goddess known as **Grandmother** noisily shaking her baggy pants, when all the mushrooms fall out. Some Japanese scientists, experimenting with electric lightning machines, have proved that there really is a relationship between fungus and thunderstorms—the gods were right!

Fly agaric (*Amanita muscaria*) contains a chemical named ibotenic acid, which attracts and kills flies, which is why it has been given its name.

Delicate **ink cap** mushrooms (*Coprinopsis atramentaria*) last only a few hours before dissolving into a puddle of brown-black fluid traditionally used as ink.

Congratulations!

Bravo for all your hard work. You now know some of the magical stories told of the world's woodlands. There are many books about trees, folklore, and fairy tales, and I encourage you to improve your magical knowledge by delving deeper into the mysteries of the forest.

Madame Volare

Glossary

Amulet—a sacred or lucky object, often a piece of jewelry.

Beltane—one of the Gaelic "calendar" festivals, marking the beginning of summer.

Canopy—the topmost layer of a tree.

Carbon-14—A scientific method of dating organic materials by measuring the amount of the element carbon left in it.

Chlorophyll—a green-colored substance in leaves that enables plants to convert sunlight to energy.

Coppicing—an ancient forestry technique that harvests wood at the base of a tree, then allows it to grow back. The tree never grows to full size, instead bearing a constant supply of young wood.

Deciduous—plants that shed their leaves in winter.

Dendrochronology—a scientific method of dating a tree by counting the rings in a cross section of its trunk.

Divination—the art of foretelling the future.

Epiphyte—an organism that lives on another living thing but doesn't take anything from it.

Evergreen—a plant that has green leaves throughout the year.

Gall—a small swollen growth on a twig or branch made by bacteria, insects, or fungi.

Germinate—beginning to grow or develop, like when a seed sprouts into a plant.

Glade—an open space in a wood or forest.

Hibernation—a state of minimal activity or sleep undergone by some animals during the winter months.

Humanoid—a nonhuman being that has human characteristics.

Nutrients—any substance that plants or animals need in order to live and grow.

Ogham—(pronounced "oh-am") an early Medieval written language using trees as symbols.

Organism—a single living plant, animal, or other living thing.

Parasite—an organism that derives some or all of its food from another living thing.

Photosynthesis—the scientific process where a plant turns energy from the sun into food.

Pollination—the process of plants making seeds by moving pollen from the male part of a flower to the female part.

Runes—an ancient alphabet of the Norse people.

Revere—feel deep respect or admiration for something.

Samhain—a Gaelic festival marking the end of autumn and the beginning of the dark months.

Sap—a plant's "blood," a nutrient-filled fluid carrying energy to a tree.

More from Madame Volare

Discover more than 50 of the world's most magical plants, as well as their uses, history, and ties to folklore.